I N THE WAK <br> tion, we hea <br> sion into two n ....argely coastal, urban party run by educated elites and a largely rural and suburban "flyover country" party composed of people who did not attend elite schools and who do not see themselves as dependent on those who did. This divide is more fundamental than mere partisan identification, as there are Democrats and Republicans in both groups.

One of the best formulations of this division comes from photographer Chris Arnade, who has spent years documenting the lives of America's forgotten classes. In his characterization, America is split between the "Front-Row Kids," who did well in school, moved into managerial or financial or political jobs, and see themselves as the natural rulers of their fellow citizens, and the "Back-Row Kids," who placed less emphasis on school, and who resent the pretensions, and bossiness, of the Front-Row Kids.

I don't want to rehash all the postelection

discussion on America's class divide, but while teaching constitutional law after the election something occurred to me: While the Back-Row Kids can elect whomever they want as their president, senators, or representatives, there is one branch of the federal government (and of all the state governments) that is, more or less by its nature, limited to Front-Row Kids: the judiciary. While someone like Wisconsin governor Scott Walker can hold office without a college degree, the judiciary is, as a practical matter, limited to people who hold not just an undergraduate, but a graduate, degree. Since the mid-twentieth century, when the last justice to achieve admission to the bar via "reading law" – that is, qualifying for the bar by apprenticing in an attorney's office rather than attending law school – Justice Robert Jackson, left the Supreme Court, the judicial branch has been the domain of judges who are not merely highly educated but educated in the particular way that law schools require. They are, in short, Front-Row Kids of the first order.

Having had that realization, my march through the decisions of the Warren Court and its successors took on a different flavor. Again and again, important decisions, seen through the lens of this class divide, look like decisions on behalf of the Front-Row Kids. Even when – as in the famous *Goldberg v. Kelly* welfare rights case – the Supreme Court looks to have been holding on behalf of poor and uneducated people, it turns out that the actual beneficiaries are the highly educated: social workers and lawyers.

In this short book, I will expand a bit on America's class division, talk about how it is embodied in the judiciary, and quickly sketch how this division seems to have affected important work done by the Supreme Court and other courts. I will then talk about how this (possibly unconscious) class bias on the part of the judiciary has inflamed America's class war, and will conclude with some suggestions for making sure things get better, or at least, no worse.

* * *

Americans have always been uncomfortable with the idea of social classes. As Paul Fussell notes in his book *Class: A Guide through the American Status System*, "You can outrage people today simply by mentioning social class, very much the way, sipping tea among the aspidistras a century ago, you could silence a party by adverting too openly to sex." In America, he continues, "the idea of class is notably embarrassing."

Class has, however, grown harder to escape. And where it used to be the case that class followed money and (secondarily) ancestry, increasingly class status in America is based on education, both its extent and its source. A hundred years ago, the upper class gained its wealth, and status, largely from its businesses: steamboats, or railroads, or coal. There was also an educated elite – usually not as wealthy, though seldom poor – who saw themselves as superior to the wealthy upper class because of their education. The rich were not always

While the Back-Row Kids can elect whomever they want as their president, senators, or representatives, the judiciary is the one branch of the federal government limited to Front-Row Kids.

the "elite," of course, as any *Gatsby* reader knows. But now the wealthy upper class has also become the educated elite. Rather than an offset to the core upper class, academia is now an adjunct to it.

That has been going on for a while. As Fussell writes, people plaster their cars with stickers advertising the schools they, or their children, attend, and do so in marked preference to advertising their churches. And the degrees handed out by these institutions —

especially the elite few, located mostly on the coasts, that constitute the Ivy League and its near kin – are so valuable that for many, acceptance in a prestigious school is an almost life-and-death affair. As Fussell puts it:

> *The psychological damage wrought by this incessant struggle for status is enormous just because of the extraordinary power of these institutions to confer prestige. The number of hopes blasted and hearts broken for class reasons is probably greater in the world of colleges and universities than anywhere else. . . . If no other institution here confers the titles of nobility forbidden by the Constitution, they do. Or something very like it.*

This is also what Chris Arnade was getting at with his division of America into Front-Row and Back-Row Kids. In Arnade's formulation, the Front-Row Kids have the following characteristics: They're mobile, global, and well educated. Their primary social network involves college and professional connections. They view intellect and intellectual achievement as the most important things in life, and view the world through that lens. Likewise, they derive meaning (and morality) from their careers and intellectual pursuits. They regard faith as irrational, and themselves as beyond petty divisions of race and religion. They see their lives as better than those of their parents and expect their children's lives to be better than their own.

For the Back-Row Kids, on the other hand, it's different. They tend to stay close to where they were born. If they have an education beyond high school, it's from a trade school, junior college, or a nonelite state school. Their primary social network exists via institutions outside of work, such as family, geographical community, and church. Faith is central. They find meaning and morality through the "decency of hard work." They have "traditional" views on race and gender. They see their own lives as worse than those of their parents and fear their children's lives will be worse than their own.

Or as Arnade simplified it in a personal communication: It's about "What is your guiding institution? Church (back row), or Academics (front row)."

After quitting a career on Wall Street and spending many years photographing and interviewing the less successful all over America, that's the division Arnade believes exists. And it's a categorization whose descriptions seem very useful to me. But I think things are even worse than Arnade makes it sound. First, the Front-Row Kids consider themselves not just winners in America but part of a *global* meritocratic elite. Where once the bonds of nationhood and patriotism might have connected them to Back-Row Kids in their own country, now they feel that they have more in common with their credentialed and successful peers in other countries than with their own less credentialed and less successful countrymen. Furthermore (as my colleague Ben Barton observes), in the years since Fussell's book was published, the institutions that bolster the Front Row have strengthened, while those that support the Back Row – the church, the family, the fraternal organizations, and other such entities – have fared poorly, as Robert Putnam, Charles Murray, and Arnade himself have documented.

Where it used to be the case that class followed money and then ancestry, increasingly class status in America is based on education.

Arnade's formulation makes clear that there are two Americas, not just in the shallow rich-and-poor sense that politicians invoke (though the Front Row is on average much richer than the Back Row) but in terms of attitudes, interests, and social connections. It also seems clear that the judiciary, at both the state and federal levels, is both made up of Front-Row Kids and likely to be more sympathetic to Front Row claims and worldviews. And unlike the other branches of government, there's not much that the Back-Row Kids can do about it through politics, at least not directly.

OUR FRONT ROW JUDICIARY

All elites create barriers to entry for their class, as those barriers are in many ways the essence of being elite. America's elite, in its combination of wealth and education, has erected several.

The first, of course, is financial. In the past few decades – coincidentally, at the same time as education has become an essential component of elitehood – the cost of education has skyrocketed, rising much faster than such other fast-rising sectors as health care and housing, as the following graphic from University of Michigan economics professor Mark Perry illustrates.

Where a few decades ago, it was possible to work one's way through school, and where even Ivy League educations were by today's standards not prohibitively expensive, nowa-

Price Changes
January 1996–December 2016

Selected Consumer Goods and Services

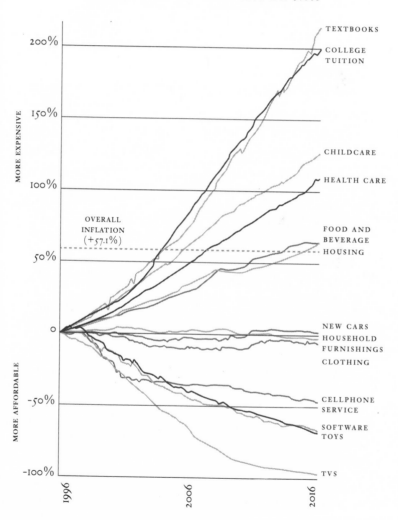

days even an inexpensive public university can cost six figures over four years – and most college students take six years to graduate.

And that's before we get to graduate degrees, now almost an essential given that college degrees are so common. And law school, of course, is a graduate program. In 2013, the average student graduating from a public law school carried $84,000 in debt, not including any undergraduate loans. Graduates from private schools carried more than $122,000. In 1985, the average in-state tuition at a public law school was $2,006. At private schools, the average tuition was $7,526. At these prices, students could pay for law school by tending bar, or working as a runner at a law firm. If they had a cushy summer job, they could probably pay for school and a nice apartment with the money they earned. No wonder a law degree was once seen as a solid investment and a great vehicle for social mobility. But things have changed.

Even the law school where I teach, the University of Tennessee, which is now featured as one of the "Best Value" law schools in America, isn't all that cheap. We're also regularly featured as one of the schools at which graduates graduate with low debt, with $66,939 being considered "low debt," where until very recently it would have been considered a staggering sum. Given that American Bar Association rules limit students' work outside of school to twenty hours per week, few students are able to work their way through law school. And, of course, *U.S. News & World Report*'s Top 14 "elite" law schools are much more expensive.

But the financial barriers are only the beginning. There's also a time barrier. College and law school are much more difficult to attend for people with small children, or aged relatives, to care for or other important family responsibilities to tend to, all things more likely to weigh upon the Back Row than the Front. And the people who do best in college – and thus are most likely to attend law schools, especially elite law schools – are often the beneficiaries of considerable parental support for earlier education, socialization, and financial help, things that are more likely to come to the children of the Front Row. Sure, some people make it anyway, but that only means that the filter isn't perfect,

The federal courts have become, in essence, our nation's moral umpire when it comes to the pressing social questions of the day.

not that it doesn't have an effect.

Then there's the social filter, which exists both before and after law school. Since the modern law school's invention by Christopher Columbus Langdell in the latter half of the nineteenth century, law schools have always emphasized teaching their students to "think like a lawyer." But now, increasingly, they teach students to think like an upper-middle-class lawyer.

Part of this is the huge amount of academic and social ranking that goes on in law school. Even today, when a bit of the bloom is off the law school rose, admission to top law schools is quite competitive. Students must jump through a series of hoops, from undergraduate grades, to high-level recommendations, to the LSAT and the "compelling" personal essay, all of which serve to reward Front Row skills and connections but penalize Back Row backgrounds.

And law itself has its own class system. Law schools are competitively ranked by *U.S. News*, and every applicant – and law school – is keenly aware of where each school fits on the list. Once students arrive at law schools, they are (except at Yale and Stanford law schools) competitively ranked by grade point average each semester. There is extensive competition for prestigious jobs and clerkships and law review slots. As Duncan Kennedy wrote in the 1970s, a lot of legal education is about the "reproduction of hierarchy."

The hierarchy is social as well as professional. As might be expected of a postgraduate professional school, the things students seek to attain are generally Front Row attainments: intellectual achievement; membership in a global profession that operates as a guild of sorts; money; prestige; and winning at whatever form of legal contest is involved. Family, tradition, local communities, and religion are not at the top of the list. ("Lawyers are the Devil's ministry," says the Devil, played by Al Pacino in *The Devil's Advocate*.) And, as *Hillbilly Elegy* author J. D. Vance, who started in the Back Row but wound up in that Front Row citadel, the Yale Law School, noted, there were a million tiny codes in the school that had to be broken to find acceptance in a place whose culture was upper middle class and above.

THE ELITE OF THE ELITE

This is the culture our judges come from. And, of course, for Supreme Court justices, well, we're talking the elite of the elite, these days. Traditionally, the Supreme Court contained former politicians (like Justice Robert Jackson, Chief Justice Earl Warren, or, for that matter, Chief Justice John Marshall). More recently, however, the Supreme Court has been entirely made up of Ivy Leaguers, mostly with backgrounds in academia or the appellate courts. (Every current justice graduated from Harvard or Yale, except for Ruth Bader Ginsburg, who got her law degree from that scrappy Ivy League upstart Columbia University – but only after spending two years at Harvard Law.) As Dahlia Lithwick recently wrote,

> *Eight once sat on a federal appellate court; five have done stints as full-time law school professors. There is not a single justice "from the heartland," as Clarence Thomas has complained. There are no war veterans (like John Paul Stevens), former Cabinet officials (like Robert Jackson), or capital defense attorneys. The Supreme Court that decided* Brown v. Board of Education *had five members who had served in elected office.*

The Roberts Court has none. What we have instead are nine perfect judicial thoroughbreds who have spent their entire adulthoods on the same lofty, narrow trajectory.

Lithwick wrote this before the accession of Justice Neil Gorsuch to the Court, but his background is the exception that proves the rule. Although some see him as bringing heartland values because he came to the Court from Colorado, he is a graduate of Columbia, Harvard, and Oxford. Only in today's Supreme Court, composed of "judicial thoroughbreds," would his resume seem even a little bit populist.

Now, at one level, there's nothing wrong with judicial thoroughbreds. They have come through an extensive winnowing process, after all. But the result is that they have been winnowed, and in a particular way. Such people may be admirable, but are they able to stand up against ruling-class, Front Row groupthink? Or even to be aware of it? To the (limited) extent that they are aware, it is in spite of their backgrounds, rather than because of them.

If the federal courts, and the Supreme Court in particular, were solely focused on technical legal questions, the dramatic gap between the backgrounds and class identities of the judiciary and those of Americans in general would be less significant. But since the mid-twentieth century, the federal courts have become, in essence, our nation's moral umpire when it comes to the pressing social questions of the day.

This use of the courts itself reflects a Front Row approach, removing decisions from the masses and placing them in the hands of educated elites. And, unsurprisingly, the courts have called balls and strikes from the perspective of the Front-Row Kids and their values, often at the expense of the Back Row. A muscular, unelected Supreme Court enforcing a "living Constitution" that conveniently reflects the prejudices of the elites, without concern for the vagaries of elections and popular sentiment, represents a particularly intrusive form of elitism. This point seems obvious enough that it probably needs no elaboration, but nonetheless, here are some observations.

Front Row Opinions

Deciding which Supreme Court opinions reflect Front Row values as opposed to Back Row values involves an unavoidable amount of subjectivity, particularly as there are no law reviews propounding Back Row legal philosophies. Most of the time, however, it is pretty easy to discern, especially as there are so few opinions that reflect the latter. But note, too, that *Front Row* and *Back Row* are not synonyms for *Left* and *Right*. Both segments are liberal about some things and conservative about others, and sometimes they even switch places: On the subject of free speech, for example, the Front Row has shifted from wholehearted support to a growing belief that free speech promotes white supremacy, while the Back Row remains generally supportive (if perhaps not as strongly so as the Front Row was back when the free speech doctrine was useful for protecting Leftist academics from Back Row objections). And not all court cases fall easily into either mold, of course. Still, there are plenty of cases where the class sympathies of the justices pretty clearly played a role.

Many moderns might think of *Brown v. Board of Education,* which ended school segregation, as a Front Row decision, but although the Front Row came to endorse the *Brown* decision, and even to define itself by its opposition to racial discrimination, at the time of the decision the Front Row was deeply divided on the issue, as were members of the black civil rights community itself. Many of them feared that Thurgood Marshall's civil rights litigators were getting ahead of themselves and risked a devastating defeat in the Supreme Court, or a destructive political backlash.

History is written by the winners, though, and *Brown* is now lionized even though its actual impact on improving education, or even integration, for African-American children has been a disappointment. Part of the reason that *Brown* did not truly end segregation in schools came from the way it was implemented: Front-Row Kids loved its unabashed proclamation of equality; Back-Row Kids were less thrilled to bear the burden of its implementation.

When it came to implementing *Brown*, it was the Back Row who mostly paid the price. Private schools, and wealthy suburbs with their own school systems, were largely exempted from the trauma of forced busing, while working-class neighborhoods received much less favorable treatment even as their betters preened, a fact that was not lost on those neighborhoods' inhabitants. This experience led to the alienation of many working-class citizens from the Democratic Party (despite Jimmy Carter's endorsement of their neighborhoods' "ethnic purity") and the rise of the so-called "Reagan Democrat" blue-collar voting bloc.

In the controversial case of *Allen v. Wright,* the Supreme Court even struck down (on highly dubious "standing" grounds) efforts to get the IRS to enforce existing laws denying tax exemptions to private schools that engaged in racial discrimination. The effect was to allow better-off kids to escape schools that were being desegregated, while leaving behind minorities and working-class whites, thus vindicating Front Row principles and leaving the Back Row with the consequences.

Forbidding states under the Warren Court to maintain geographically drawn districts that violated the equal-size principle greatly strengthened urban areas, which tend to be Front Row strongholds.

Expanded freedoms in the sexual arena also mostly served the Front Row agenda. In *Griswold v. Connecticut,* the Supreme Court struck down a Connecticut law banning sales of birth control drugs or devices to everyone, even married couples, leavening its decision with some talk about the "sacred precincts of the marital bedroom." But within just a few years, the Court, in *Eisenstadt v. Baird,* decided that the right to use birth control should not be relegated to "marital privacy" after all, but rather should be expanded to include the right of "the *individual,* married or single" to choose whether or not to have sex and to bear and beget children. Later, in *Carey v. Population Services International,* the Court extended this freedom to minors as well.

The Back Row was now just as free as the Front Row to use birth control, and did, but the real impact of this Court-induced change was to make it easier for the daughters of the Front Row to delay marriage while pursuing extended educations and careers. It was possible to remain single, and even to have sex, while pursuing college or a postgraduate degree before the *Griswold* decision and its progeny, but it was a lot easier to do so afterward.

And these things became easier still once *Roe v. Wade* established the principle that not only would birth control be available but that the right to terminate a pregnancy at any time in the first two trimesters would also be available as a backstop. Many of the arguments in favor of this decision were explicitly based on the way an unexpected child could derail a woman's career plans, arguments that implicitly assumed that everyone had career plans of the sort that, in fact, were a staple of Front Row, not Back Row, lives.

It's possible that the late-'70s/early-'80s "yuppie" – young urban professional – phenomenon of postponing raising children in favor of pursuing a career would have been less pronounced if these "reproductive rights" cases had not made extended dating and schooling, and delayed marriage, so much easier. (This extended schooling – and school-related dating — also facilitated a drastic increase in "assortative mating," where there was a historically unprecedented level of marriage between members of the Front Row, concentrating income in two-earner professional households and further increasing the distance between the Back Row and the elite. Where once a Front Row boss might marry a Back Row secretary, now Front Row only married Front Row, and Back Row folks were on their own.)

Later cases involving gay rights, *Lawrence v. Texas* and especially the *Obergefell* same-sex marriage case, reflected Front Row priorities almost exclusively. There are, of course, plenty of working-class gays, but the gay marriage movement in particular was very much a Front Row priority. A *New York Times* article after *Obergefell* notes that the District of Columbia – a very Front Row place indeed – is very different than America at large:

These days, justices are more likely to work and socialize with openly gay people than most Americans are. That is partly because 10 *percent of*

adults who live in the District of Columbia say
they are gay, lesbian, bisexual or transgender,
according to a February Gallup poll. That is a
much higher percentage than in any state. Law
schools and the legal profession have, moreover,
been particularly welcoming to gays and lesbians.

Even in decisions that would seem to favor the Back Row, it often turns out that the Front Row is the real beneficiary. In the famous case of *Goldberg v. Kelly,* for example, the Supreme Court found that welfare recipients whom the welfare agency determined were ineligible enjoyed a constitutional right to a hearing before their benefits could be terminated. (Previously, they had the right to a hearing, but only the right to reinstate benefits *after* termination, with back pay, if it was found the termination was wrong.)

When I attended Yale Law School, *Goldberg v. Kelly* was still considered one of the great accomplishments of the Supreme Court, praised in pretty much every class I took – even my Admiralty class. (Yes, really.) But who does the ruling actually help? Well, unless – as seems doubtful – taxpayers are willing to send more money to welfare agencies in order to pay for hearings, the likely impact is that the same total amount of money will be appropriated, but now some not-insignificant portion of it will go not to provide benefits for poor people but rather to pay for the lawyers, social workers, clerks, and others needed for additional due process hearings. The net effect is that money that used to go to poor people is now going to people with jobs and credentials: the Front Row.

It didn't take long for the Supreme Court to realize the potentially far-reaching impact of *Goldberg,* and to limit it to its facts. But the case in which it did so, *Mathews v. Eldridge,* is itself a slap in the face to the Back Row with its belief in the "decency of hard work." In *Eldridge,* the Court found that a recipient of disability benefits was *not* entitled to a pre-termination due-process hearing of the sort that welfare recipients were entitled to under *Goldberg.* The Court provided a number of reasons for this, none of them especially convincing (among other things, it said, people who lost their disability benefits could always apply for welfare). But the outcome was a situation in which people who don't work — welfare recipients — are entitled to a hearing, while people who can't work — disability recipients — are not. As a thought experiment in one of the classes I teach, I ask students to imagine the "attack ads" that could have been made regarding this result if the Supreme Court had to run for reelection. But, of course, it does not. If it did, the result would likely have been different.

And speaking of elected bodies, the Supreme Court amplified Front Row power to an unappreciated extent in its decisions in *Baker v. Carr* and *Reynolds v. Sims.* (The Reynolds here is no relation.) Previous Supreme Courts had refused to get involved in the "political thicket" of redistricting and apportionment, but the Warren Court rushed in where those earlier courts had feared to tread, establishing the "One man one vote" principle that all districts should be of equal size,

The judiciary is one branch of the government that looks a lot more like an Ivy League faculty than like America as a whole.

so that voters would have the same proportional power, and forbidding states to maintain (as the Federal Constitution requires for the US Senate) geographically drawn districts that violate the equal-size principle.

The Court could have addressed the very real misbehavior here in a less intrusive fashion – for example, by ordering states to follow their own state's constitutional rules on reapportionment, which were being flagrantly ignored. Instead, the sweeping rule it issued had the effect of greatly strengthening urban areas, which tend to be Front Row strongholds, at the expense of rural areas, whose politics tend to be more traditional and Back Row influenced. One suspects that this was not an accident, but rather the motivation, or at least a motivation, for the approach the Court chose.

In media law, too, the Front Row has received judicial support. The pivotal libel case of *New York Times v. Sullivan* held that public officials – later broadened to "public figures" of any kind – could not win a libel case without showing "actual malice" on the part of the defendant. ("Actual malice" doesn't actually mean malice, but rather knowledge that the published statement was false, or issued in reckless disregard as to whether it was false or not.) The result of these decisions was, in effect, a subsidy to media companies, whose libel risks (and insurance premiums) were drastically reduced. It also meant that juries, the only Back Row institution in the judicial system, had far less power in libel cases. Perhaps coincidentally (but perhaps not), trust in the press has fallen steadily since the *Sullivan* ruling freed media organizations from previously existing legal accountability.

Decisions in other areas have similarly

empowered the Front Row over the Back Row: Increased efforts to promote the "separation of church and state" meant that many traditional displays of religion, important to the Back Row and with a long history in America, were suddenly offensive to the Constitution. Increased protection for materials previously considered obscene inevitably, despite references to "community standards," involved a homogenization in which it seemed impossible to imagine that material acceptable in New York could be considered obscene in Des Moines, since the imagining was done by judges whose standards were closer to New York's. And judicial protection for a right more highly valued by the Back Row than the Front Row – the right to keep and bear arms under the Second Amendment – was slow and grudging in comparison to the judicial protection offered for many rights not specifically mentioned in the Constitution at all, and more highly valued by the Front Row crowd. Nor are these the only such cases; I will leave the rest, as the old mathematics textbooks used to say, as an exercise for the reader, to discover on his or her own.

None of this is to say that these decisions were all wrong. I actually agree with many, and perhaps most, of them. In particular, I have written at some length in defense of the Court's opinion in *Griswold*. But few of them were so clearly correct that they *had* to come out as they did, and in most it is easy to see the Court elevating the Front Row's concerns and minimizing, dismissing, or outright ignoring those of the Back Row.

Bringing Diversity to the Judiciary

So far, I have noted that our country is increasingly divided into the spheres Chris Arnade has labeled "Front Row" and "Back Row." I have also noted that the Front Row character of our judiciary, and especially the Supreme Court, has become much more pronounced in recent years, and that the decisions of the Supreme Court often seem to be driven as much by the shared beliefs and viewpoints of the Front Row as by anything else. What does this mean?

Well, for one thing it means that a Supreme Court (and a judiciary in general) that is overwhelmingly dominated by viewpoints from one side of our society's great divide is likely to be insensitive to viewpoints held by those on the other side. Indeed, it may well be the case that the beliefs of the Back Row aren't just being overridden, but rather that the justices aren't even aware of those viewpoints at all. A court that is unaware of, or that disregards, the values and viewpoints of half the country is very likely to rule in ways that inflame existing divisions, and perhaps even create new ones. There may be cases where that's appropriate – as the Romans used to say, "Fiat iustitia, ruat caelum," or "Let justice be done though the heavens fall" – but even in such cases, it would be better if the Court fully appreciated what it was doing. If, as I noted earlier, the courts were focused on narrow, technical legal issues, this would matter less, but the judiciary, and in particular the Supreme Court, has occupied a much greater role than that for longer than I have been alive.

And, of course, the legitimacy of the judiciary suffers, too. Americans have been lectured for decades about the importance of diversity, about the need for institutions that "look like America," and so on. Yet the judiciary is one branch of the government that looks a lot more like an Ivy League faculty than like America as a whole. This has not escaped people's attention, particularly as the Court renders decisions that reach directly into their daily lives. (And it doesn't help that – as with Ivy League faculties – the justices' written output is overlong, turgid, and self-referential, a far cry from the crisp, punchy, accessible output of the Marshall Court.)

So what is to be done? Well, there are drastic remedies available if people think the problem is severe enough: An elected judiciary (or at least an elected Supreme Court) would give the Back Row the same power to influence the federal judiciary's makeup as it has in the legislative and executive branches. What's more, the need to run for election, and possibly reelection, would ensure that justices paid far more attention to the views of nonelite Back Row Americans. It's true, of course, that the Constitution provides for no such thing, but if the problem is sufficiently serious an amendment is not out of the question. And, after all, many states do just fine with elected judiciaries. There are issues, of course, but it's not as if appointed judiciaries are themselves free of politics, or political influence.

Even without a constitutional amendment, we could resurrect Colonial practice (or emulate the practice of some contemporary nations) and appoint some nonlawyer judges. The Constitution contains no requirement that federal judges and justices be attorneys; that has always been the practice, but we're constantly hearing that established customs need to change to meet the needs of today, and perhaps what we need today is a judiciary that is less inbred.

Writing in the *Stanford Law Review* a decade ago, Harvard law professor Adrian Vermeule argued for just that: nonlawyer justices on the Supreme Court. As Vermeule observed:

> *If there were some controlling rule of law requiring all Justices to be lawyers — in either the modern or the older sense — then the argument I offer here could just be cast as an argument for changing that rule. Still, it is worth pointing out that there is no such rule; nothing in the Constitution, statutes, precedents, or legal traditions bars the President from nominating nonlawyers for the Supreme Court.*

So we could either hold elections for Supreme Court justices, which would require a constitutional amendment, or we could simply appoint some nonlawyer justices, which would be a big departure from history — there has never been a nonlawyer on the Court — but would not require a change to the Constitution. Either step would certainly diversify the Supreme Court beyond the current judicial thoroughbred monoculture.

Beyond these rather sweeping changes, there are less drastic things that we can do to effect this type of change. The fact that we

---

If the Supreme Court in the past flourished with justices who had been politicians and criminal defense attorneys, it could surely flourish with such justices again.

---

have judicial thoroughbreds dominating appointments today has to do with two things: One is the elevation of credentialism in contemporary society over the past few decades to a level that is without any precedent in American history. The second is the role of the judicial confirmation wars, in which a gold-plated resume (coupled with a lack of controversial public statements) is seen as an essential part of getting nominees past the Senate. Ever since President Nixon's nominees Clement Haynsworth and G. Harrold Carswell were rejected by the Senate, with Carswell openly characterized as "mediocre," presidents have tried to ensure that their nominees were immune to such a charge.

But it cannot be the case that there are no nonmediocre candidates outside the profiles of today's judicial thoroughbreds. There are plenty of first-rate people out there in the world who went to law school somewhere other than Harvard or Yale (or, in the case of Ruth Bader Ginsburg, two years of Harvard and then a degree from Columbia). If the Supreme Court in the past flourished with justices who had been politicians, criminal defense attorneys, and so on, it could surely flourish with such justices again. Its writing might even improve.

Certainly plenty of able Supreme Court justices have come from places other than the Front Row. The last justice to have "read law" (qualifying for the bar by apprenticing in an attorney's office) with no other formal education was James Francis Byrne, named to the Court by Franklin Roosevelt in 1941. Also named to the Court in 1941 was Justice Robert H. Jackson, regarded as one of the most intellectually formidable justices of the twentieth century, who had one year of legal education at Albany Law and read the law in 1913. Chief Justice Warren E. Burger, named to the Court in 1969, had done two years of law school at the St. Paul College of Law (later becoming William Mitchell and then Mitchell Hamline) and got a law degree in 1931, but he received that degree without ever having attended college.

In the short run, I would encourage presidents and senators to look at appointing – both to the Supreme Court and to the federal judiciary generally – people with experience as state judges, preferably from states where judges have to run for office. There are plenty of first-rate people who fit this description, men and women who would make fine judges, and who would be at least somewhat more sensitized to the world of the Back Row than the usual lineup of judicial thoroughbreds.

Likewise, perhaps it's time to reach beyond Harvard, Yale, and Columbia law schools as a source. There are many fine lawyers and judges who are graduates of state law schools, or private schools outside of the Ivy League. The Supreme Court would function at least as well, I suspect, with a few graduates from places like Texas, or Kansas, or Pepperdine.

Earlier generations of justices – like earlier generations in general – contained far more military veterans. The US military is probably the most diverse institution in America in very many ways, and a nominee with military experience – especially if it involved actual work with troops in the field or sailors at sea – would understand a lot about America that your average Harvard Law grad missed.

Speaking of earlier generations of justices, perhaps Congress should reinstate the practice of riding circuit. For many years, Supreme

Court justices filled their off months on the Court by traveling around and sitting on appellate courts in various locations. A revival of this practice would expose the justices to much more of America, especially if the justices sat as district court judges occasionally. The justices would probably complain about the workload, but given that the Supreme Court hears roughly half as many cases as it heard a few decades ago, and that justices are well equipped with clerks, support staff, and office equipment, the burden should not be excessive.

A Supreme Court That Looks like America

These are all (aside from the election of justices) changes that would not require a constitutional amendment, or even legislation. They are, rather, suggestions that the president, and the Senate, should step back from the judicial thoroughbred template that has governed the Supreme Court (and increasingly other judicial) appointments for several decades and look at different types of candidates who, while still very capable, would bring a broader social awareness to the work of judging.

Although the politics of confirmation fights, as noted earlier, are probably against me, I hope that these suggestions will get some attention. As our society is more and more riven by the Front Row–Back Row divide, I think that it would be very helpful to have a Supreme Court that looks more like America. Such an outcome would, I believe, be better for the country, and better for the long-term legitimacy of the Court itself.

First American edition published in 2018 by Encounter Books, an activity of Encounter for Culture and Education, Inc., a nonprofit, tax exempt corporation.
Encounter Books website address: www.encounterbooks.com

Manufactured in the United States and printed on acid-free paper. The paper used in this publication meets the minimum requirements of ANSI/NISO z39.48–1992 (R 1997) (*Permanence of Paper*).

FIRST AMERICAN EDITION

LIBRARY OF CONGRESS
CATALOGING-IN-PUBLICATION DATA
IS AVAILABLE

Reynolds, Glenn Harlan
The judiciary's class war / Glenn Harlan Reynolds.
pages   cm. — (Encounter broadsides ; 54)
ISBN 978-1-64177-001-9 (pbk. : alk. paper) —
ISBN 978-1-64177-002-6 (ebook)
LC record available at https://lccn.loc.gov/2018000155

10 9 8 7 6 5 4 3 2 1